Persuading People To Be Good

Alasdair MacIntyre's Three Rival Versions of Moral Enquiry *and Why We Should Read It*

Joshua Rey

GW00692037

GROVE BOOKS LIMITED
RIDLEY HALL RD   CAMBRIDGE   CB3 9HU

Contents

Dedication

This booklet is dedicated to the memory of Bishop Lesslie Newbigin, who suggested and encouraged its preparation. It is intended to be a contribution to the continuation of his work .

Throughout the text, any general statements using male pronouns are assumed to be equally applicable to both sexes.

The Cover Illustration is by Peter Ashton

First Impression January 1999
ISSN 0951-2659
ISBN 1 85174 393 6

1

Introduction

The Great Problem of the Late Twentieth Century

The problem of our times is that we cannot talk to one another. We do not just disagree about what is true, we disagree about what is truth. How often have you met with the following rejoinders, or ones like them: 'That's just what you think'; 'Why should I?'; 'That may be true for you but it's not true for me.' They are unanswerable—and one hears them all the time. They are the sticking point in any attempt to evangelize. And they are at the heart of our age's profoundest social ills.

It need not be thus. However deeply rooted in our late-twentieth century outlook on life these attitudes are, however far we may be from sharing the same vision of what a compelling argument is, however little we may be prepared to meet one another in argument, however we may think that mere argument can resolve nothing—it need not always be thus. We have got into this sorry frame of mind as a result of a particular history. We are not stuck here. The history of how we got here is at root a history of ideas. If we understand this history we can put ourselves in a position to move on, to somewhere better.

Alasdair MacIntyre's Book

My purpose in this booklet is to introduce an important book which can offer some help. The book is *Three Rival Versions of Moral Enquiry* (London: Duckworth, 1990, £12.95, 236pp). There is no substitute for reading this excellent and rewarding book in its entirety, but this booklet may be of assistance in providing a route map and setting the book in context. The author is Alasdair MacIntyre, a moral philosopher. Whilst the book contains a diversity of interesting ideas, I want to concentrate in what follows on one particular set of themes which I think can be found in it, namely:

1) Each of us has his own criteria for working out what is true and what Truth is.
2) When two people with different conceptions of rationality have a conversation they never get anywhere. For you to convince me I not only have to accept your arguments, I have first to accept your criteria for what is a good argument.
3) To bridge the gap between these rival versions of moral enquiry we need the patience and humility to enter into the worldview of those who have a different scheme of rationality so we can challenge their adherence to it.
4) This patience and humility is the backbone of an outlook on life—a

fundamentally Christian one—which itself constitutes one such rationality, but one which can show itself superior to the others because it answers questions which they pose for themselves but cannot answer.

What This Has To Do With the Price of Cheese

MacIntyre's book is addressed to an academic audience.[1] Although high tables on every continent are riven by the arguments he deals with, most of us in the lay world would not immediately know what all the fuss was about. Nonetheless it is my purpose in this booklet to summarize MacIntyre's contribution to resolving these disputes and to suggest that his ideas are important to all of us, not just because if you prick a professor he bleeds but because there is a trickle-down effect whereby, over many years, an idea that has power in the ivory tower comes to have power over the rest of us. Understanding the history of ideas can help us to understand the condition of the world we live in.

It is easy to assume that somebody who is not in our own sphere of rationality is not in any sphere of rationality at all. The Romans called the tribes beyond the imperial borders barbarians, derived from the Greek *bárbaros* meaning foreign, *of unintelligible speech*. Because they did not speak Latin the Romans thought one could not speak with them at all. We should always try to avoid this error, and much of what MacIntyre says to his academic audience can be very helpful to us in the attempt.

Plan of the Booklet

The remainder of this booklet breaks down in the following way. Chapters 2 and 3 cover the argument of the book itself. Chapters 4 and 5 suggest ways these arguments are important in our daily lives, 4 dealing with what I have learnt from the book about the origins of our difficulties and 5 covering some solutions it offers. There would be nothing to stop you reading 4 and 5 first if that would help whet your appetite. I must make it clear that whilst 2 and 3 are intended as an introductory summary route-map of the book itself,[2] 4 and 5 are my own attempt to apply MacIntyre's observations about the history of ideas to tangible problems of our own time and neither of these chapters is meant to represent MacIntyre's own views.

---

1 It is a revised version of his 1988 Gifford Lectures, in which a distinguished thinker is invited to Edinburgh to discuss natural theology.
2 Hence only original insofar as I have misunderstood MacIntyre.

2
The Three Rival Versions Described

Outline of the Book

Our failure to convince one another in argument seldom results from a failure to argue convincingly or to advance the best evidence, but often from fundamental disagreement about what is a convincing argument, about what constitutes evidence—about what we are really doing when we argue. I can bring forward numerous good arguments which would convince anyone who already agreed with me about what a good argument is. But if we do not agree about this fundamental point I will never convince you on any of the substantive questions we are talking about. Rational argument gets us nowhere if we disagree about what being rational involves.

MacIntyre describes three different schemes of what rationality is which have been and are very influential in the Western world, the eponymous three versions of moral enquiry. In summary, they are:

1) Encyclopaedism, which found its highest expression in the Ninth Edition of the *Encyclopaedia Britannica* and of which Adam Gifford, whose will paid for MacIntyre to write his book, was a typical adherent;

2) Genealogy, the ideas of Nietzsche and his descendants (I use the word 'descendants' advisedly), classically articulated in *Zur Genealogie der Moral*;

3) Thomism, a mediaeval tradition first seriously given modern expression in Leo XIII's encyclical *Aeterni Patris*.

MacIntyre describes each of these schemes and what someone who inhabits it is likely to say and do; discusses ways someone who lived by one scheme could attempt to argue with, rather than simply fight, someone in another; and finally organizes a league play-off between the three in which Encyclopaedism comes off worst, having played two and lost two, whilst Genealogy beats Encyclopaedism but loses to Thomism which takes the grand slam.

In the remainder of this chapter I introduce the three rival versions; chapter 3 covers the play-off.

What Do Encyclopaedists Believe?

MacIntyre would phrase this differently. He would say 'what *did* Encyclopaedists believe?' He thinks nobody really takes the Encyclopaedist view seriously anymore: 'The key beliefs and concepts which they shared…are what separate us from…them,'[3] whereas the texts of Genealogy and Thomism 'are able to play a part in defining the conflicts of the present in a way that Adam Gifford's will is not.'[4] I am inclined to believe that Encyclopaedism is alive and well outside the universities (and is what most people, if they consider the question, think they believe in) if for no other reason than because compared to its two rivals it is much easier to describe.

It is what one naturally thinks of as 'rationality.' It is the view that underneath all the different branches of knowledge and enquiry descending from physics through economics to the difference between right and wrong, there is a regular crystalline structure of fact. There is a pattern out there in the universe that everything fits into. We cannot see it all but that is only because we have not looked carefully enough.

Pursuing knowledge is like tuning a radio; there are many stations different only in having different content, alike in being broadcast in the same way and from similar places with similar apparatus. At first our clumsy crystal sets can only pick up something fuzzy and incomprehensible on Deutsche Rundfunk, but as we progress we get a wider spectrum and in the end we will hear all the stations with equal, perfect clarity. Our contribution to the advancement of knowledge is to build better radios. It is a high and noble endeavour, the end result of which is a programme guide showing where on the dial you find chemistry, where psychology and where moral philosophy. This guide is called the Encyclopaedia.

The crucial points are these: that knowledge is out there waiting for us, inert but independently existing; and that the history of ideas is the history of a progress from mistaken and superstitious apprehension of this knowledge to the clearer, more elegant and more unified conception we have today, and on to the perfectly unified, all encompassing understanding we will have the day-after-tomorrow. The history of the world is a progress from superstition through religion to knowledge, in which we get closer and closer to the point where we know everything, where we will stop.

And I think this is in fact what most people think they believe in. They may, if you listen to them, display different views about what constitutes a proof or a good argument or a convincing piece of evidence; but they will still imagine that knowledge is the same for everyone: not merely that there is a consensus about what truth is, but that there is only one, inert and independently existing, truth.

So much for the Encyclopaedist outlook. To summarize its essential features:
1) all knowledge is objective, that is to say independent of us but inert;
2) all knowledge can be addressed and apprehended in the same way using

3   *Three Rival Versions of Moral Enquiry*, p 23.
4   *ibid*, p 25.

the same tools;

3) the history of ideas is a more-or-less continuous history of progress.

What Do Genealogists Believe?

Nietzsche's title tells us everything we need to know: *On the Genealogy of Morality*. What is right and what is wrong are not questions towards whose answers we have slowly but continuously progressed since classical times. They are not questions that ever could be answered in that way. The history of how we got to our current outlook on morality followed no predetermined path, was not about laying bare some preexisting fact. No, history is just *what happened*. It is not like finding a fossil inside a rock, when you tap away gently at the stone and eventually the shape of the ammonite becomes clear; it is like carving, rather clumsily, the shape we choose.

This, I take it, is why Nietzsche talks about genealogy rather than, for example, development. You can trace the ancestry of ideas; you can look at the historical events which caused each generation to have slightly different ideas from the one before; but this is not a development towards a given point, whose path is determined by something which is already there. Knowledge is not about apprehending something outside the knower; it is something the knower does for purposes of his own.

So far this is a negative statement, addressed to people who think truth is objective. But Nietzsche himself puts a particular spin on this view. He has a specific idea of what purposes the knower is serving when he 'does' knowledge. He does not think history just happened; he thinks there is a story behind it, and this is the story of the Will to Power.

Nietzsche says that what people really want is power over one another. They can get it in simple, straightforward ways, like hitting each other with sticks; on the other hand if they are sneaky, they go to the trouble of building up, over centuries, a complicated structure of ways of acting and speaking which, through customary acceptance and by being surrounded with awe-inspiring symbols, command obedience on a grand scale.

Then, instead of having to train themselves up to fighting fitness, all they have to do is go around effetely arguing with the people they want to dominate, whom they thus dupe into subservience. Nietzsche thinks this is a dastardly trick and his plan is to expose it. He wants to make us authentic and to free us from the undeserved domination of limp-wristed moralists who are all mouth and no trousers, but still get away with murder by exploiting the spurious ideological superstructure that we call morality.

But, though the Will to Power was a central concern for Nietzsche himself, this aspect of his thought is not crucial in the Genealogist worldview for MacIntyre's purposes. One could sign up for the Genealogical outlook on what we are doing when we talk about truth and morality, without subscribing to

Nietzsche's particular view of history. You could tell a story about how we got where we are today which would still be a story of ancestral descent rather than upward progress, but not the same blood-curdling story that Nietzsche tells.

In setting out the Genealogy stall MacIntyre mingles the original ideas of Nietzsche with those of his descendants, particularly Foucault and Deleuze. This contemporary Genealogy is different from Nietzsche's in two ways: it is less bloody in outlook; and it is a general attack on the Encyclopaedic view of all areas of enquiry in the humanities—and potentially the sciences too—and not just on the soft target of moral philosophy. It is this gentler but more endemic Genealogy which MacIntyre puts into the ring against Thomism. The argument between them is carried on in terms of rather neuter entities like 'unity of project…a deliberating, purposeful self…logic…identification …contradiction …appeals to evidence,'[5] and on this territory Genealogy loses.

What Is Thomism?

Thomism is to the modern reader the least familiar of the three modes of moral enquiry. One thing that immediately makes Thomism hard to grapple with is that we usually expect something called Robinsonism to be the philosophical system of Robinson, whereas in the case of Thomism it is not like this. Thomism is not the philosophy of Thomas Aquinas, but rather the outlook of the philosophical world in which he worked and to which he made a big contribution. It is, as MacIntyre says, an error to treat Aquinas 'as presenting a finished system whose indebtedness to earlier writers is no more than an accidental feature of it.'[6] This gives a clue to what Thomism is about.

Aquinas's great work was his synthesis of the two contending philosophies of early second millennium Europe, the incumbent Augustinianism and the challenger Aristotelianism (or, arguably, his incorporation of the latter into the former), which he accomplished by repeatedly following this procedure:

1) using the techniques and preoccupations of Aristotelianism to pose a problem for itself;
2) showing how that problem could be incorporated into a bigger picture in which it could be solved;
3) by so doing, demonstrating the superiority of the particular scheme of rationality within which he was working and which came to bear his name, that is, the Thomistic tradition.

In this process, Aquinas was forging Thomism; but he was also doing Thomism. For this is a procedure rooted in the Thomist conception of knowledge: that

5   ibid, p 55.
6   ibid, p 74.

moral enquiry is a craft, carried on within a tradition. To practice a craft, you first find a master to work for. Then you suspend disbelief and submit yourself to the master's teaching until you start being able to do some of the things he can do. Then you are in a position to try out your own ideas. But by then you are contributing something to an existing structure rather than striking out on your own.

Knowledge is something that happens in a particular community with a particular history. Indeed it could not happen in any other way. Our capacity to know things is something we have to learn, not something ready formed waiting to be fed with the objects of knowledge. Ignorance is not just a matter of lacking contact with the objects for knowledge; it is an incapacity for apprehending them. This leads to a paradox: I cannot get to know anything until I first know *how* to know.

This is a puzzle to which the Thomist has an answer, namely that we begin to know by submitting to authority. In practical terms, this authority is ultimately God speaking through the Bible and proximately the tradition of understanding the Bible in which one grows up.

I think this has two main consequences for epistemology[7] which I summarize so as to accentuate the contrast with Encyclopaedism:

1) knowledge is outside the knower; but
2) it is not inert.

Finally, this is true both of moral enquiry as it goes on in the universities, and also of how one conducts one's own life. So the rules for living a moral life, like the objects of knowledge, are not hanging in the ether ready to be adopted the moment I open my ears to them. No, in order to be a good person I must first submit, and then go through the arduous process of learning. There are, of course, moral rules. But if all I had was the moral rules written down as an *aide memoire* I could no more act well than I could become knowledgeable by being given the *Encyclopaedia Britannica* without having first learnt to read.

So there are at least two surprising things about Thomism:

1) knowledge and goodness are acquired in similar ways;
2) the way one acquires them is through submission to authority and learning within a tradition.

---

7 Forgive me if you do not need to be told this, but I want to make it clear that 'epistemology' means nothing more than 'what one believes about how one knows things.'

3

The Three Rival Versions Pitted Against One Another

Nietzsche **Versus** *Adam Gifford*

The first fixture is bit of a mismatch and is not treated in detail. The pretensions of the Encyclopaedists (Henry Sidgwick, author of the Ethics article in the *Encyclopaedia*, memorably referred to the history of progress 'from Socrates to myself'[8]) are inflated enough to be easily punctured.

It was against exactly this kind of person, at this very point in time, that Nietzsche was writing, and his negative epistemological argument is telling. The kernel is what one might call the 'pantomime argument': Adam Gifford says 'knowledge is of something outside the knower, existing timelessly and pursued for its own sake' to which Nietzsche answers *'oh no it's not.'* Nietzsche's attack was timely, and succeeded in erasing the Encyclopaedist mode of moral enquiry from the academic world.

I think, however, as I have said, that Encyclopaedism lives on in the hearts of all good men on the Clapham Omnibus. This points to a defect in Nietzsche's attack. One very effective response to the pantomime argument is, after all, the pantomime counter-argument: *'oh yes it is.'* Short of carrying his programme through to its obvious conclusion and starting a proper punch-up, Nietzsche has abandoned any attempt to convince the Encyclopaedist of his own failure in terms the latter can understand. And of course in practice Nietzsche did not start punch-ups.[9]

Since he declines to convince us by force, we either see Nietzsche's point or we do not. University Encyclopaedists did see it, and died out; but for the rest of us Encyclopaedism has not been exploded. When it suits us we question all kinds of received wisdom, and in this we are Nietzsche's debtors. But it often does not suit us to question Encyclopaedism. Nietzsche gave us the tools but no motivation to use them and so, in the wider world outside the university, I am inclined to declare a draw.

Aquinas **Versus** *Adam Gifford*

In the first of the contests where Thomism is involved we see a better standard of play. The pantomime argument stays on the bench throughout. Instead, MacIntyre tries to do what Aquinas attempted with the rival moral schemes of

---

8   *ibid*, p 186.
9   William Shirer reports a remark of Bertrand Russell on Nietzsche's famous line 'Goest thou to woman? Do not forget thy whip!' Russell said: 'Nine women out of ten would have got the whip away from him, and he knew it, so he kept away from women.'

his own era: to show that Thomism can deal with questions that Encyclopaedism must ask itself but cannot answer.

He begins with an entertaining discussion of the Encyclopaedists' attitude to the taboo rules of Polynesia, which appeared to hold a fascination for them probably attributable to their desire to throw off their frock coats and run naked into the equatorial surf.

To the Encyclopaedists the taboo rules were a set of random prohibitions. But this was an error. If the Encyclopaedists had followed the taboo rules whilst wearing their frock coats in Edinburgh then the rules would indeed have been nothing but random prohibitions. For the Polynesians, however, taboo performed an important function as the glue that held together their larger social structure. The Encyclopaedists may be forgiven their error because by the end of the nineteenth century this structure had passed into history. In a short time after the arrival of Europeans, all the social arrangements that were supported by and gave meaning to the taboo rules were grubbed up. All that was left was the rules themselves.

MacIntyre's killer argument is that the Encyclopaedists' own approach to morality is like the taboo rules after the arrival of the Europeans. The starting point for Encyclopaedist ethics is the idea that moral rules exist in a well-ordered system standing, as it were, on the same bookshelf as physics, chemistry and so on. Moral philosophy was meant to be a science. For their morality to be legitimate and mature, not mere custom, it had therefore to be the highest expression so far of a continuously improving enquiry into an unchanging subject matter.

They took this subject matter to be the pretheoretical judgments of the plain man. The task of the moral philosopher was to come up with a scheme which, from a few simple axioms, could consistently derive the moral judgment with which the plain man, given sufficient time for reflection, would agree.[10] In practice this scheme was a modified Utilitarianism under which we were to pursue Universal Happiness but, because some of Utilitarianism's more extreme conclusions are too much for the man on the Clapham Omnibus to stomach, we were also allowed to pursue our own happiness.

The trouble was that sometimes you would be faced with a situation where Universal Happiness required one course of action and personal happiness another. Sidgwick thought this a mere technical matter. He and his predecessors were on the right track but not quite clever enough to make it all work; one more heave would do it. MacIntyre's point is that it was not flawed execution

---

10 I may add that this idea of moral philosophy was still being studied and taught in Oxford in the late 1980s. Whenever one learnt about one moral scheme or another, whether it was Utilitarianism or Rawlsian justice or whatnot, the test was always whether one could come up with a counter-argument of the form 'but in these circumstances your system means we would have to act like this, and we obviously don't want to do that.' The 'obviously' was the most contentious but one of the least remarked upon words, which I now recognize as the Encyclopaedist appeal to the plain man, alive and well in the drawing rooms of North Oxford.

that caused the project to fail; the project itself was a mistake. For the moral judgments that Sidgwick wanted to undergird were not the distant objects of a quasi-science, they were the survivals of an earlier way of life which had disappeared. Encyclopaedists were the inheritors of a botched and misunderstood Thomism in the same way as the contemporary Polynesians, with their seemingly random taboo rules, were the inheritors of a complex society that had made sense in its own terms but had been destroyed by contact with Europe.

The Encyclopaedist, then, fails because he wants to live by the leftover rules of Thomism without rooting them in their native tradition. The reason this does not work is that the moral rules are secondary; what is primary is the practice of virtue. This is both more rigorous and more flexible than the following of moral rules that went on in the elegant Edinburgh homes of the Encyclopaedists. It is more rigorous because it is a way of life, something you do all the time, not just at moments of moral tension, and something you have to work at, rather than reading it off from an article in the *Encyclopaedia Britannica*.

But it is also more flexible because, having acquired these skills by the traditional craft-learning process, the Thomist can deal with each moral problem in its own terms. As rules of thumb he uses moral prohibitions much like those of the Encyclopaedist; but when these conflict, his well-practised virtue enables him to judge correctly. The Encyclopaedist's moral rules are like circuit diagrams; Thomism is the skill of the engineer without which the diagrams are useless.

To summarize why the Encyclopaedist loses to Thomism:

1) he is committed to certain moral rules;
2) he also wants to root his moral rules in his overall worldview, which teaches that morality is akin to the natural sciences; but
3) because they are survivals from a radically different worldview, moral rules cannot be accounted for in this way, and in fact will not work when used in this context.

So the Encyclopaedist has a dilemma. Either he has to say that his moral rules do not matter, or he has to say that he does not know why he does not tell lies but he is just jolly well going to refrain from doing so anyway, which is to admit that his overall scheme of rationality does not work. Fortunately for the Thomist, he is too well brought up to do the former.

Aquinas Versus *Nietzsche*

MacIntyre has one rather simple anti-Genealogical argument which, for good reasons, he rehearses frequently in different forms. The version I liked best rests on the behaviour of Paul de Man's apologists. De Man was a Yale deconstructionist, avowedly descended from Nietzsche. After his death it came to light that he had, in the early forties, written some articles supporting the Nazis, for a journal in his native Belgium. His academic descendants took it on themselves to construct a defence, arguing that in his later writings de Man had, in moving away from the theories that underlay the offending articles, implicitly criticized and repented of his earlier views.

The problem with this is that Genealogists are committed to disowning their pasts. Indeed de Man, in the very writings that were meant to be his implicit repentance, asserted, if I understand the obscure passages MacIntyre quotes, that there is no difference between truth and fiction. So either there is no reason to apologize because he did not really write what he wrote, or there is no possibility of making a real apology out of his later, somewhat fictional, writings.[11]

Here MacIntyre is fleshing out the following skeletal argument:

1) to take responsibility for one's past, one has to believe that the self continues through time and is in essence the same thing now as it was then;
2) although the physical body is an important part of what it is to be a person, one has to be able to distinguish a body constituting a self from a mere automaton;
3) among the ways we do this is by saying that the self is the thing which can be held accountable for its actions by other people; but
4) Genealogists think that all this talk of being held accountable is a fiction, a mask over a much more *ad hoc* power struggle.

The conclusion is that the Genealogist rejects what MacIntyre thinks is one of the central constituents of the self. Without it, the idea that I am the same person I was last year no longer makes any sense. MacIntyre then goes into a variety of different ways that Genealogists in practice do still talk and act in a way that presupposes at least their own continuity through time, if not that of the people they are writing about—one example being the de Man story.

To summarize the summary:

1) the avowed reason for doing Genealogy is to emancipate the Genealogist from the spurious tyranny of received wisdoms; but
2) this means there must be a person who is in important respects the same person before and after emancipation;
3) Genealogy has no place for such a person.

This is pretty much an *ad hominem* argument, which is no bad thing if you have to do with Genealogists. As the taxi driver said, 'it's the only language they understand.' What MacIntyre says against Genealogy boils down to *'well, you*

---

11 At least, I think that is the point, but what is one supposed to do with a gobbet like 'demystification of an organic world postulated in a symbolic mode of analogical correspondences or in a mimetic mode of representation in which fiction and reality could coincide'?

can say that's how things are, but you don't actually want to live like that, do you?' His skill is in saying it in ways that are effectual in disturbing and challenging the people he is addressing. Doubtless his meticulous explication of what real Genealogists actually say and do works as well as anything else not prohibited by law in expunging the tedious evil of post-Nietzscheanism.

The only argument I can think of on these lines that is not *ad hominem* is this: the inability of created men and women to live out the tenets of Genealogy points to their having been created with a different worldview in mind—not just that by failing to act out their ideas they are being inconsistent, but that by being *unable* to act out their ideas they show their ideas to be *false*. This of course is not an argument that would convince a Genealogist.

4

What MacIntyre's Ideas Can
Tell Us About the Roots of Our Era's Problems

An Introductory Anecdote

During the time I was reading MacIntyre I was once on a train which stopped at, if I remember correctly, Wimbledon.[12] There was a man on the train who did not have a ticket. The guard was asking him to pay and, the man refusing, to leave the train. I stood up in the hope of supporting and encouraging the guard and the man at once turned to me and said 'If you want to take me on—outside; otherwise keep out of my business because you ain't got nothing to say to me.'

This was puzzling and troublesome. I did not want to have a fight with him but I did not want to ignore the whole affair. Normally in this kind of dilemma I resort to a kind of talking which is really fighting, consisting mainly of aggressive reprimands. Luckily on this occasion, under the influence of MacIntyre and Aquinas, I had the presence of mind to answer 'but those aren't the only options: you could tell me why you think it's all right to do what you're doing and I could tell you why I think it's wrong, and in the end either I'd agree you were right or you'd agree you were wrong.'

Well of course it did not change anything. There was still a scrappy argument that ended with the man getting off the train with lots of cursing and bad feeling. It may be that my refusing to have a fight—verbal or physical—planted or nurtured a tiny seed but I do not flatter myself that it was a life-changing event. It is, however, a handy incident to illustrate the parlous state we have got into.

In the good old days people usually robbed because they wanted what you had, they did murder because they were angry with or afraid of the victim. Today, although many of these traditional motives endure, there is another, and in the long run more powerful, force at work. It is the Nietzschean rhetorical question *why not?* There is nothing new in bad behaviour; indeed in comparison with former centuries ours is not a violent or lawless age. What is new is that bad behaviour is less and less acknowledged to be bad. People who act badly are less likely now than in the past to realize that they are acting badly.

They will not say 'you may think I am doing wrong but here are some reasons why you are mistaken.' They will seldom even say 'I am doing wrong but I am going to go on doing wrong.' And they will even be unlikely to try to cover up what they are doing. Covering up bad behaviour is not, of course, a sign of

---

12 I should emphasize, however, that the line is immaterial.

health; but the decay of any will to cover things up is a sign of the particular disease of our times. Not that we do more and worse wicked acts, but that the resources to correct ourselves have withered away.

The most surprising thing about my encounter with the man with no ticket was not that he betrayed no contrition. Few of us have the capacity to be contrite immediately we are convicted of doing wrong—on the contrary, being shown up as in the wrong is, there and then, a barb to stimulate defiance. No, the noteworthy things were

    1) he did not show any sign of wanting to justify himself; and

    2) nobody else in the train wanted to get involved.

Both these are illustrations of the extent to which Nietzsche's ideas[13] have become diffused throughout our country, to our loss.

The Trickle-Down Effect in Intellectual History

It may seem contrived to attribute an unexceptional *contretemps* on a suburban train in 1990s Britain to the thought of a nineteenth century German lapsed professor. But many broad social movements have had their roots in narrow intellectual concerns in the universities of a past era. The very phrase 'trickle-down effect' first saw the light of day in the *Antioch Review* of Summer 1944,[14] an American academic journal of sociology and political economy. Now it is widely understood. A new concept has coalesced, which allows and encourages us all to think in a slightly different way. Whether we believe it works or not, our thinking about economics and the distribution of wealth is indelibly marked by our having the use of the concept of the trickle-down effect.

It is a good parlour game to think of academic usages which have trickled down in this way; that it is a parlour game you can play for a long time shows how powerful this phenomenon is. It is an open question whether great thinkers actively shape the times or are simply better than others at catching the trend in its infancy,[15] but either way we can learn a good deal about ourselves by seeing how their ideas have trickled down to us.

Often the most influential trickle-downs have been from thinkers working outside the mainstream of the universities. Darwin and Freud spring readily to mind: think how differently you would see the world if you had never heard of evolution or the unconscious. Nietzsche is yet more powerful because what he bequeathed us was so much simpler. It was an idea with no name, which each

---

13 If you are reading the booklet from back to front, this would be a good moment to review the section beginning at page 7.

14 *OED.*

15 For my own part I am inclined to think that the mood of the times limits the range within which a thinker can have new ideas but that big ideas at the extremes can, in subsequent generations, move the ends of the range: like amoebae, human societies move from the edges, and the greatest thinkers are often at the extremes of thought. But this question, fascinating though it is, is not central to our discussion.

of us can imagine is his own. It is not a concept that can be named and attacked; it is an attitude of mind that has been unleashed among us and, like the grey squirrel, gone so much native that we can no longer remember the indigenous creature it supplanted.

We Are All Nietzscheans Now

Let me give some practical examples of how I think this trickle-down has worked, starting with the two interesting features of my encounter with the man with no ticket.

1) He did not show any sign of wanting to justify himself. Nietzsche's big idea was that when we use moral language we are doing something dishonest. 'Truth,' 'goodness,' 'duty' and so on are nothing but grand totems, hallowed by time and customary acceptance, which we respect, and which have power over us, because we have forgotten that there is nothing behind them. To use moral language 'is to give evidence of membership in a culture in which lack of self-knowledge has been systematically institutionalized.'[16] It is to be deformed and inhibited; it is a failure of the will; it is in the end contemptible.

   This idea is now common property. It is the source of the slightly creepy feeling that one gets when one starts out to give moral reasons for what one has done; the feeling that the brave thing to do is to let the actions stand on their own. The man with no ticket said 'you ain't got nothing to say to me.' This might be paraphrased as: 'you are implicitly trying to challenge the rightness of my actions; but any such challenge involves the use of moral language; and since I make it my business to be free from the psychological repression that makes people take that kind of language seriously, we may as well dispense with the discussion altogether.'

   In a way, this is of course fanciful. I do not really think the man with no ticket had Nietzsche's arguments at his fingers' ends in that way. Nietzsche's thought is widespread because it has trickled down, not because it has been learnt. We understand it inarticulately and incompletely; moral language still has power and currency. But what Nietzsche's ideas have given us, and in particular what they gave the man with no ticket, is the sense that this power and currency is oppressive and unwarranted; that submission to it is cowardly; that to speak moral language is to crush one's true nature.

   In the past the man with no ticket might have offered violence because he felt unable to justify himself. I believe in our time he offers violence because he believes, in a deep but unspoken way, that if he tries to justify himself he sells his birthright for a mess of pottage.

2) The other interesting thing was that nobody else in the train wanted to get involved. The corollary of 'why should I?' is 'why shouldn't he?' It is no

---

16 *Three Rival Versions of Moral Enquiry*, p 35.

business of mine. The only thing that is my business is *my* business. I think that deep down we have learnt Nietzsche's lesson, that when we admonish our fellow man our motive is that we want power over him. A hundred years ago the streets of England rang with the cries of self-righteous Victorian Gents bellowing 'you there, stop that at once, what do you mean by it?'

I am not a tremendous fan of the Victorian Gent because I incline to believe that quite often he actually was just interested in power over his fellow man. A hundred years ago I should have cheered Nietzsche for taking him down a peg or two. But today we have lost that capacity for saying what is right and what is wrong without worrying about our motives. This self doubt is what keeps the commuters nestled in their newspapers when the guard needs their support.

And I Do Mean All of Us

And of course, this was not an unusual episode. You have doubtless met with the same sort of thing. Maybe you have, like me, in a more genteel way perhaps, been on the other side. Throughout our life as a nation this goes on, large and small, rude or gentle. Let me give a brief illustration from the big end of the spectrum.

In the last few decades it has become less and less acceptable to question the righteousness of what we glibly call market forces. As a former merchant banker I am among the last to argue against capitalism. I firmly believe that what Hayek called 'the extended order of human co-operation'[17]—the market economy—is the bedrock of any economy that is going to keep us all fed and clothed; and that because it is uniquely able to do this, we need to let it flourish but shoulder the burden of understanding and defusing its malign side-effects. But I think the reason why our world so adores market forces has little to do with this understanding of their genuine virtues. No: the reason we have learnt to stop worrying and love the market is because it meets the need of our Nietzschean age.

A few years ago Michael Heseltine became slightly more notorious than he already was when he asserted that paying one's invoices only on presentation of the final demand was nothing but good business practice. But he was not saying anything particularly startling. It is nothing unusual in business to work strictly to the letter, rather than the spirit of an agreement. Indeed this is often justified as part of the duty one owes the shareholders. Likewise, to lie when necessary, so long as one cannot be caught out, is certainly, in my experience, an unremarkable practice in the banking world.[18]

When businessmen argue for ethical behaviour it is usually on the grounds that it is good for business to be seen to be ethical. We add up the cost of acting

---

17 Friedrich Hayek, *The Fatal Conceit* (London: Routledge, 1988).
18 I used to work for a man who sold bonds. People prefer to buy bonds when they think lots of

rightly and we compare it to the benefits of possessing an ethical reputation. Forgive me if you or one of your friends is a truly moral businessman or woman answering to a higher law. There are such people and they are to be cherished. But for the most part our culture teaches that there is something contemptibly weak, something hairshirty, something of the sneak and the swot, about asserting moral values as primary in the economic world. Lunch is for wimps and nice guys come last.

The reason we love the market is that it provides us with a fence along the edge of this abyss. As children of our time we have imbibed the sense that doing Right, being considerate and moderating our greed are not imperatives but luxuries. But as humans made in the image of God we have at the backs of our hearts a feeling that if we all throw ourselves into the Nietzschean project with the gusto its founder required then the world we like to live in will break down. We recognize that the fruits of compromise and co-operation are really rather nice.

The splendid thing about the market is that it permits us to be unreconstructed Nietzschean Wills without immediately losing the advantages of an organized civilization. It gives us a framework in which we can abandon conscience without immediately descending into barbarism. Greed is good (if only in the narrow sense that it conduces to an increase in the common wealth) and because this maxim conduces to a strange but powerful form of co-operation, it gives us a sense of security when we opt out from the broader moral world and live the lives Nietzsche has fitted us for. This is not to say that Nietzsche himself would have liked our commerce-obsessed age any more than he took to the conventional morality of his own: only that his thought, in the perhaps debased form in which it has trickled down to us, has made a hole in our moral world which we patch with market forces.

So much for supporting examples. To summarize the argument so far:
1) our Nietzschean inheritance has lumbered us with the profound belief that when we argue about morality all we are doing is trying to have power over one another;
2) this idea has, over the last hundred years, come to permeate our common life;
3) the result is a widespread disinclination to behave gently and a corresponding disinclination to admonish one another for this failing.

This is a bit glum on its own. But if we understand the history which brought us to this pass we will see that people do not inevitably act like this; and we will be better equipped to change our sorry condition.

other people want to buy them too: so this man had a lie which he regularly told, that there was 'a bit of interest from the Middle East.' 'Keep it general,' he would say, 'don't mention any names but hint at the Kuwaitis—always gets 'em going.' Another colleague recalled a discussion about what to present to a client at which a senior banker came out with the memorable observation 'in this case I think we can get away with the truth.'

5
Putting MacIntyre's Ideas to Work

Three Introductory Disclaimers

First: I do not offer MacIntyre as a universal panacea. Our social ills have a variety of very deep roots of which Nietzschean Genealogy is only one. Each problem needs attacking from all sides, and MacIntyre does not have a single shot solution even for the problems he *does* discuss. We will not be free with one bound. There is no cunning wheeze. The final victory will not come in our lifetime. Nonetheless, what MacIntyre does offer is no small thing. It took us a long time to get into this state, and it is not to be expected that we would come up with a special trick which would get us out of it without equivalent effort.

Second: what I say here about the ways MacIntyre can help deal with our social and spiritual problems is as much what I have read into his book as what I have read out of it. I do not claim MacIntyre's authority for what I say; and it would be remiss of you to content yourself with gathering my impressions of MacIntyre, rather than affording yourself the benefit of gathering your own. An introductory booklet is no substitute for the book itself, and the remainder of this chapter presents only the edited highlights of what I have gathered from MacIntyre's book. I divide these highlights as follows.

1) *About preconceptions.* There is no neutral position. Everybody begins with a leap of faith, but some people do not know it. If you do not know your own preconceptions you cannot effectually defend the worldview which they underlie. If you do know somebody else's you can have a better crack at arguing with him. This is in the following section.
2) *About the relationship between politics and epistemology.* Our ideas about how people should live together need to be supported by a more general worldview. We court disaster if we try to have just the political ideas; in particular the secular humanist values of tolerance and respect are undermined by the wider secular humanist idea of what truth is. This is the main burden of the third and fourth sections.
3) *About how to argue with people one disagrees with fundamentally.* Points (1) and (2) are little more than intellectual curiosities unless we can argue constructively with people who have different ideas about what a good argument is from our own. Surprisingly, this turns out to be possible. This is covered largely in the last two sections.

Third: at some points I talk about the problem of social disintegration and the problem of evangelism side by side. I keep them together because evangelism, or the spread of faith by other means, is an essential part of addressing the big social problems. This is not a casual truism, but a vital truth, one for which I find grounding in the arguments MacIntyre deals in, some of which I will mention. But I also want to affirm that the reason to believe in God is that God is, not because a widespread belief in him would make the world a better place. The arguments I offer are no more use for evangelism than theodical arguments are. Justifying God's ways to man removes reasons *not* to believe, and my arguments may likewise stop the atheist dismissing the gospel as irrelevant. But it is only grace that will bring him from respect to belief.

The Beginning of Wisdom

The secular worldview's tragic flaw is its spurious desire to be neutral. You can be a neutral referee in a game where the teams agree on the rules. You can arbitrate neutrally between two referees who disagree if you know what constitutes a good decision. But below a certain depth neutrality stops. At the level of epistemology, you *cannot* be neutral: your theory of knowledge is what you use to decide whether something is true or not. It is the highest court of appeal and cannot rule on its own decisions. You either believe it or you do not, but your belief or otherwise cannot be supported by arguments.

The Encyclopaedists missed this point, and imagined themselves, in contrast to every other people of every other age, to know about the world without making a leap of faith. This blindness (which one might unkindly call arrogance) is bad for two reasons:

1) it is a barrier to hearing the gospel;
2) it is also a handicap for today's secular liberal in defending his, in many ways attractive, moral values.

What *are* the presuppositions of the humane atheist on the Clapham Omnibus? In philosophy departments it is understood that the Nietzschean *'oh no, it's not'* argument is as telling on any sphere of human life as it is on its original target, our common morality. Fifty years ago it was commonplace to say 'it all depends what you mean by right and wrong.' Next in sociology we realized that to call someone working class or Irish was to take a position rather than to state a fact. Now everyone is entitled to his own take on world history, and on the edge of the hard sciences, archaeology and biology have become legal battlegrounds.

But outside the universities the typical atheist or agnostic (and often Christian) has, as to the physical world, presuppositions that are essentially Encyclopaedist, and run on the following lines:

1) the evidence of our senses is for the most part reliable—if I see a cow there is a cow there;
2) our memories are largely reliable—if I recall having seen a cow last week then there was a cow there;

3) the future typically resembles the past—the cow will not randomly vanish or turn into a table when I turn my back, and more generally if in the past event A has always been followed by event B then it is fair to expect that if we get event A today we will probably also get event B;

4) the observations and reasoning of others, based on these first three principles, are also to be believed—books on cows are reliable.

If this sounds like a heavy load of principles to carry around on the Clapham Omnibus, find a thinking lay atheist, ask him to tell you some things he believes about how the world works, and then ask him to tell you *why* he believes them. I think he will pretty soon come up with something a lot like my points (1) to (4).

And the trouble with these points is that they leave no space for the gospel. Call me a religious maniac if you will, I do not think that any worldview that rules out the Resurrection (*cf* point 3) is a good worldview. This betrays my own pre-rational commitment, and will not convince an atheist that his worldview is wrong. But what one *can* do by laying bare his pre-rational commitments is convince him that he *has* some.

This conviction can be an important step on the road to faith.[19] If you can convince the atheist that he has already submitted to *one* authority (that is, to the implicit preconceptions of the Enlightenment) then you challenge him to tackle the question what is the *right* authority.

Cargo Cult Morality

The liberal atheist's mistaken preconceptions are plainly a problem for evangelists. There is also, however, an important though less obvious respect in which they are a problem for the liberal atheist himself—namely, they fail to provide a foundation for his ethical values.

I am not alone in wanting the man without a ticket to be polite to the guard. Christians and liberal atheists both value civil peace and gentleness. But the liberal atheist is in the position of Henry Sidgwick. He thinks his beliefs should be founded on 'objective' premises like points (1)–(4) above, but his objection to fare dodgers is not this kind of belief at all. If he attempts to derive it from his 'objective' premises he will fail.

The Encyclopaedists mistakenly imagined themselves to be occupying a neutral position without pre-rational commitments. Nietzsche exploded this pretension, and without its foundation stone, Encyclopaedist thought has come tumbling about our ears. All the humane ideals typical of the Enlightenment at its best—progress and tolerance, co-operation and respect for the individual—cannot now be advanced as universal ideals, but merely as personal preferences.

---

19 I write as a satisfied customer.

Indeed, the contemporary liberal humanist is probably in a worse position than Sidgwick who, being a proper Victorian gent, doubtless had a bullheaded sense that bad behaviour was bad behaviour. The humane atheist on the other hand is likely to have taken enough Nietzsche with his mother's milk that he may be shy of even *asserting* that the fare dodger should obey the guard (much less arguing for the point). Who is to say he did not *need* to avoid the fare, that from his own point of view it was not wrong to be rude?

Much noble intellectual effort has been devoted to coming up with a liberal social theory that would meet this difficulty. The famous and beautiful system of John Rawls is a good example.[20] He develops a theory of justice based on the following thought experiment. Imagine yourself behind a 'veil of ignorance,' where you do not know whether you are man or woman, black or white, rich or poor. Now consider what form of government you would want to live under. The result is a society in which inequalities of wealth can only be justified if they increase the size of the pie so that the really poor are better off.

Robert Nozick had a similar procedure that came to more *laissez faire* conclusions.[21] You think of what institutions of government would arise as the result of the informed consent of all participants. This is an old game which Bentham and Mill were the first to play—to come up with a theory which will be neutral and uncontested because it keeps all the men on the Clapham Omnibus happy. Without exception, all these theories either have been found to bristle with exceptions to the point where they say nothing, or have had to admit that they smuggle in some non-neutral assumption—for example about what the man on the Clapham Omnibus really needs.

And even if, which it never could, such a theory held together in its own terms, it would still tend to undermine itself in practice. Liberal theories of justice are based on some variation of taking what we all on average say we want and trying to secure it for us in a logical fashion. But if one sees enough of these theories march past the saluting base one notices that the thing they have in common is not the ethical behaviour they are meant to underpin, but the fundamental faith in the individual will. *What I want*—that's the thing. And if we sign up for this, pretty soon some bright spark gets the idea that he could get a bit more of what he wants by some well-calculated skullduggery. Let me summarize:

1) liberal social theories like to think they are based, as the whole of Encyclopaedist thought wants to base itself, on neutral ground;
2) but actually you cannot say anything without some preconceptions;
3) to the extent they *do* say something, liberal social theories are founded on

20 John Rawls, *A Theory of Justice* (Harvard, MA: Harvard University Press, 1971).
21 Robert Nozick, *Anarchy, State and Utopia* (New York: Basic Books, 1974).

preconceptions about what the typical individual wants;
4) this is not neutral at all: and worse, it encourages a view that the will of the individual is paramount, which is just what the Genealogists (against whom these theories should be buttressing us) have been saying all along.

Now, this failure of liberal social theories is rooted in the history of ideas. Basically, MacIntyre's story is that liberal social theories are attempts to find foundations for ideas in one worldview which in fact can only be successfully rooted in another, the one that gave them birth. The contemporary moral sense is a cargo-cult survival of a much older common culture, namely the Thomist tradition and the Christian faith of which it is a part. In short, the liberal atheist's ethical outlook is doomed without the gospel.

The Gospel As the Basis of Civil Society

The belief that the strong should not take from the weak is not a universal belief in history, as a cursory reading of Greek myth shows. No, the reason we Europeans believe that the strong should not take from the weak is because ours is (or was) a Christian continent. That is not to deny that there are cultures in other parts of the world which teach that robbery of the weak by the strong is bad, but our beliefs on this score are shaped by Christianity.

Now, as I argued above, the atheist cannot just say 'thanks for these good ideas about morality which I herewith adopt—but please do not trouble me with all this God business.' For if he wants to make these beliefs stand up in a secular context he either simply asserts them—and in short order the argument becomes a trial of strength—or he attempts to build them into some secular scheme of rationality, such as the liberal theories of justice mentioned above, which staves off disaster by temporary obfuscation but does not avert it. When it comes down to it, he has no answer to the Nietzschean *'why not?'*

Thomism on the other hand has never denied that a world without preconceptions is a world without friction, in which no-one can ever get moving. There is no beating about the bush. Thomism does not duck Nietzsche's fast ball but strides out of the crease and hooks it confidently:

1) humans do not work properly, and in fact do not really exist, separately from one another;
2) to get on together they have to acknowledge and act on their duty to one another and to their community;
3) this duty is not a list of rules but rather a tradition of behaviour and belief which is a lifetime's study;
4) to begin this learning one must first submit to the authority of the tradition, which is ultimately biblical and divine.

A striking feature of this worldview is its outlook on authority. These days we reckon authority mostly a bad thing. We suspect the motives of people who undertake the responsibility of exercising authority. Indeed, it is telling that we normally talk about them 'claiming the right to exercise authority,' and we can be contemptuous of those who submit to authority—their submission marks them out as lacking gumption. MacIntyre on the contrary makes the point that without some kind of authority we will never get anywhere. If you do not believe your teacher knows what the letters mean you will not learn to read.

Tradition also gets a better write-up than one is accustomed to. Doing things the way they are commonly done is not laziness or self-serving conservatism, it is about being involved in the life and growth of one's community. We should not denigrate authority and tradition. The important thing is to submit to the *right* authority and live in the *right* tradition.

This outlook on life, which of course requires a great deal more development than I have space and you have time for, offers a foundation for many of the social values which we and the liberal atheist both hold dear. On this foundation they can be defended against the Nietzschean attack.

The Encyclopaedist and the Genealogist social theories are alike in taking as their starting point the primacy of the individual will. Encyclopaedists do so implicitly and with the best of intentions, 25 Genealogists with a confident flourish. This is why the Encyclopaedist is on a loser when he tries to answer the Nietzschean question posed by the man with no ticket—*'why shouldn't I?'* The Thomist on the other hand does have an answer, which boils down to *'because God says you mustn't.'* Of course, this does not on its own make the man get off the train. But it has this advantage over the humane atheist's approach: it does not undermine itself.

Arguing Across the Gulf

The argument above is typical of the strategy of Thomism. There is a deficiency in your way of thinking: the Thomist persuades you to recognize that deficiency in your own terms; he then shows you how Thomism can meet the deficiency. When a Thomist has overcome you in argument you are not destroyed so much as annexed. This is MacIntyre's answer to the problem of how you argue with somebody who has a different view of what argument is from your own.

In the preceding section this argument went on at a very general level, the level of abstraction that is quite familiar from MacIntyre's book. I want to give now an example of how it might be made to work at the level of detail we usually work at. Above (page 18) I argued that the reason we are so keen on the free market is that it salves the symptoms of our Nietzschean disease. I want to pick up this discussion again now and suggest how one might use MacIntyre's Thomist strategy to attack the axiom 'Greed is Good.'

To begin with, let us assume that we do not offend God by being greedy. This is not a great assumption (because it is wrong) but it is the assumption on which Rational Economic Man proceeds. Let us say for the sake of an argument then, that being kind, renouncing wealth and telling the truth to one's disadvantage are leisure activities like golf and snorkelling which we do at weekends if they are the kind of thing we like. They do not contribute to the well-being of the world in the same way as reducing the cost of capital does.

A theme in recent economic research,[22] however, is an attempt to quantify in money terms the value of trust as an economic lubricant. The theory is that without trust in business relationships transaction costs go up, squandering the golden eggs as the goose lays them. But a culture in which people trust one another is not something we can take for granted. It is what you might call a piece of moral infrastructure—it has been built, and we can pull it down or allow it to collapse through want of maintenance. When it is finally exhausted the only way to keep businessmen from cutting one another's throats will be a gross proliferation of law and lawyers. This will be jolly expensive.

Hence Greed is not ultimately Good even in its own terms—it undermines and exhausts the patrimony of trust and shared values that lets the wheels of the money-machine go round. In the long term the greedy worker works to rule, the greedy buyer has to tie up each deal in acres of contract, the greedy banker pulls the rug from a shaky company that could have been saved. In each single case, the individual involved is doing the best thing for himself and yet is not doing the most constructive thing for our common future—not only by then and there increasing the cost of doing business, but by further undermining the culture of trust.

No amount of statutory regulation can make it profitable to behave well each time. What we need is *personal* reasons to act rightly. We need a world where we know our generosity will not be imposed on and where selfishness is punished not by law but by conscience.

Note what has happened in this argument:

1) I accepted, for the sake of the argument, that just because something was wrong did not mean you should not do it;
2) I also cited economic research which did a funny thing: it evaluated trust in money terms;
3) having done these two things I was then in a position to say to the Nietzschean free marketeer that, though he and I disagree about the meaningfulness of moral terms, still, a worldview in which those terms do have a meaning can solve some of the problems that his worldview sets but cannot solve.

---

22 *eg Cambridge Journal of Economics*, March 1997, Special Issue on Contracts and Competition.

This is, I think, an example of how MacIntyre's Thomist strategy can work in practice. And the essential element here was to take the trouble to see the world from the other fellow's point of view without losing sight of his being wrong. It is not enough to give him arguments that convince me—I have to go to the trouble of reading the *Cambridge Journal of Economics* so I can begin to find arguments that will convince him. Arguing across the gulf is not impossible, as one might have thought—but it is hard work.

Eating with Publicans and Disputing with Pharisees

Note point (2) in the section above. If somebody proposed to you to demonstrate the financial value of trust, you might well say 'don't be ridiculous—isn't it *obviously* valuable?' And you might also have said 'some of the *effects* of a culture of trust may have a financial value, but trust itself has a value which in its very nature cannot be added up in money.' Both these insights are right, but they cut little ice on the dealing floor. Recognizing this is the key tactic of the Thomist approach, of which MacIntyre is a master.

Refer, please, to the discussion of the failure of Genealogy on page 12 above. MacIntyre's arguments do not conclusively demonstrate by an elegant Aristotelian procedure why the Genealogist proposition is false. Instead they tease and tickle the Genealogist with haunting echoes of his own diffuse and allusive style. I want to say 'that's not an argument.' Certainly it would not convince me. But then I am not a Genealogist.

MacIntyre, also not a Genealogist, has made a considerable personal effort to inhabit the Genealogical worldview, to 'learn [its] idiom…from within as a new first language, much in the way that an anthropologist constitutes him or herself a linguistic and cultural beginner in some alien culture.'[23] As a result he is in a position to argue with them in a way they may respond to. His book is not just about how to conduct an argument between two opposed modes of rationality; it is a living part of that argument.

This should be a familiar tactic to Christians for it was also, of course, what Christ did. He spoke the demotic of his day but said something new in it. He did not scorn the company and habitat of publicans and sinners but went cheerfully into it to show them a better way of life. And on the other hand when he argued with the scribes and the teachers of the Law he could be as rabbinical as you could wish. It must have been quite an effort to keep telling the same story in so many different languages, but it was the only way to reach the people who needed reaching. And on a larger scale, the Incarnation itself gives us the greatest example there could be of taking the trouble to speak the language of those who need to hear the story.

In our own day and place the people who most need to hear the story are

---

23 *Three Rival Versions of Moral Enquiry*, p 43.

not, as they were in Jesus' time, persons of strong religious beliefs who were marching boldly down a variety of blind alleys. No, today the most common attitude one meets with is one of wishing to sit completely still at the junction of all paths. Of course, we know that there is no such neutral position. But unless we trouble to understand the belief that there is such a place, and the desire to occupy it, and the contempt and outrage that our stepping away from it sparks off, then we will be hard put to keep the attention of the atheist for long. If we do not understand his Encyclopaedist view of miracles then we will not be able to talk to him without sounding superstitious and primitive. If we cannot feel the force of the Genealogist's question 'why shouldn't I?' then we will never convincingly answer it.

The most powerful thing MacIntyre has to offer us is this simple but challenging tactic: don't tell; show. This entails doing three things:

1) making the effort to speak the language of the person you are confronting, even at some personal cost;
2) persevering with argument despite its appearing to be ineffectual;
3) living what one believes in as well as describing it.

These are hard to do. In my confrontation on the Portsmouth train with the man with no ticket I had the presence of mind to do (2) and was, thereby, to some extent doing (3). (1), at which I failed, is a lifetime's study. In trying to get them right I have been aided by MacIntyre both by his giving profound reasons why they are worth doing, and by his giving an example of the skill and dedication involved in doing them. In the course of his book he does not just tell us to make the effort to show rather than tell; he actually then and there is himself doing just that.

After all, the book was originally a lecture series given to an audience undoubtedly stiff with neo-Nietzscheans. It is a real piece of preaching to the unconverted, an argument across the gulf. MacIntyre's humility in making the imaginative effort that put him in a position to have this discussion is the strongest of many reasons why his ideas and his book should recommend themselves to us.